# knights & armor

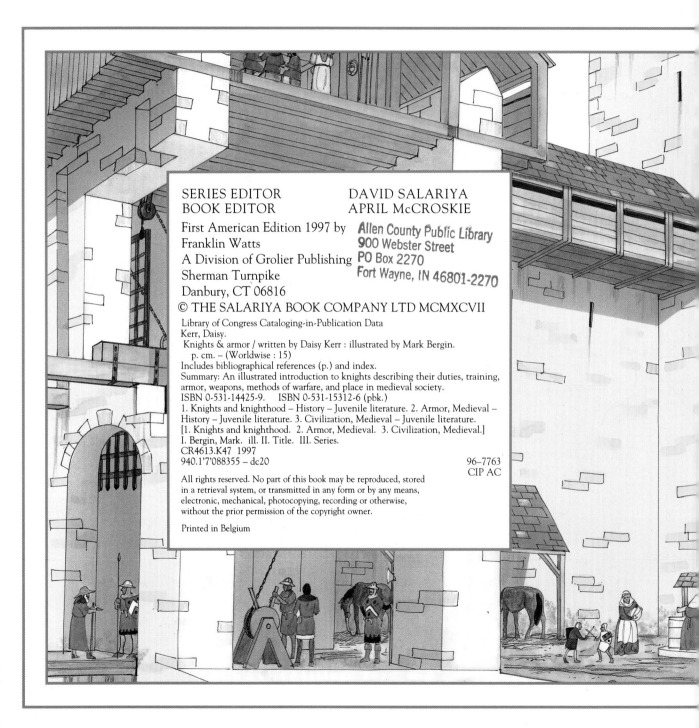

SERIES EDITOR      DAVID SALARIYA
BOOK EDITOR        APRIL McCROSKIE

First American Edition 1997 by
Franklin Watts
A Division of Grolier Publishing
Sherman Turnpike
Danbury, CT 06816

Allen County Public Library
900 Webster Street
PO Box 2270
Fort Wayne, IN 46801-2270

© THE SALARIYA BOOK COMPANY LTD MCMXCVII
Library of Congress Cataloging-in-Publication Data
Kerr, Daisy.
 Knights & armor / written by Daisy Kerr : illustrated by Mark Bergin.
   p. cm. – (Worldwise : 15)
 Includes bibliographical references (p.) and index.
 Summary: An illustrated introduction to knights describing their duties, training,
armor, weapons, methods of warfare, and place in medieval society.
 ISBN 0-531-14425-9.    ISBN 0-531-15312-6 (pbk.)
 1. Knights and knighthood – History – Juvenile literature. 2. Armor, Medieval –
History – Juvenile literature. 3. Civilization, Medieval – Juvenile literature.
 [1. Knights and knighthood. 2. Armor, Medieval. 3. Civilization, Medieval.]
 I. Bergin, Mark. ill. II. Title. III. Series.
CR4613.K47 1997
940.1'7'088355 – dc20                                    96–7763
                                                         CIP AC

Printed in Belgium

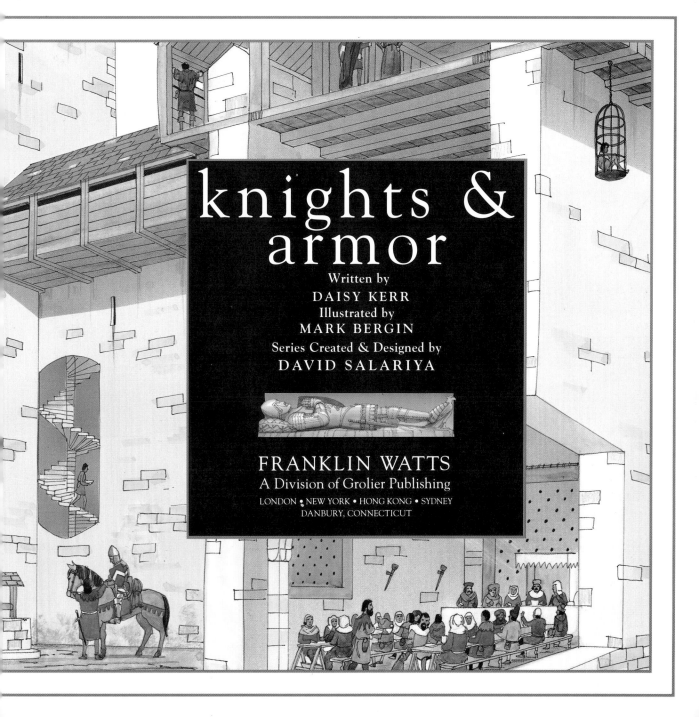

# knights &
# armor

Written by
DAISY KERR

Illustrated by
MARK BERGIN

Series Created & Designed by
DAVID SALARIYA

## FRANKLIN WATTS
A Division of Grolier Publishing

LONDON • NEW YORK • HONG KONG • SYDNEY
DANBURY, CONNECTICUT

# Knights were warriors who rode on horseback and fought with swords and spears. They were almost always men – women were not normally trained to fight.

Knights lived in the Middle Ages, between A.D. 1000-1500. Most knights came from noble families. Some were rich and powerful, and lived in splendid castles. But some were rather poor.

Kings and princes were trained as knights too. At the end of the Middle Ages, some knights became professional soldiers, fighting for anyone who would pay.

# The feudal system

began in 9th-century Europe. It worked like this. Lords helped the king fight. They took bands of soldiers with them to war. Later these soldiers were called "knights."

Knights showed loyalty to the king and to their local lord. In return for this loyalty, knights were given castles and big estates in the country. Estates were farmed by people called peasants. Knights promised to protect peasants in return for their hard work.

**Knights** acted as judges in the local courts. A knight might also use the court to punish any peasants who had not been doing their work properly.

**The estate's farm** produced all the food the knight and his family needed. A knight collected money, rent, and taxes from the peasants. In wartime the peasants stayed within the castle walls for safety.

# It was a knight's duty to fight

bravely whenever the king or lord needed his

help. Knights had other duties, too. They

were expected to be courteous to their

enemies, treating prisoners

humanely, and not

attacking civilians. Sadly, in wartime, these rules were often ignored.

Knights were meant to be chivalrous – respectful and loving – to women. It was their duty also to protect the Church.

**A king** or great lord housed, fed, and clothed his private army of knights and foot soldiers. They were always ready to ride with him to war. He might provide them with uniforms or special badges, so they could easily tell apart friends and enemies.

1160    1265    1330    1400    1450

# Knights wore armor made of metal, padded cloth

and leather. The earliest "chain-mail" armor, from
around 1200, was made of small iron rings, worn over
a padded tunic, or aketon. Around 1300, knights fixed
solid steel plates to their tunics to protect their chest,
shoulders, and legs. Knights covered their heads with
metal helmets. By 1400, armor was made of steel plates
riveted together. It was hot and heavy, but strong.

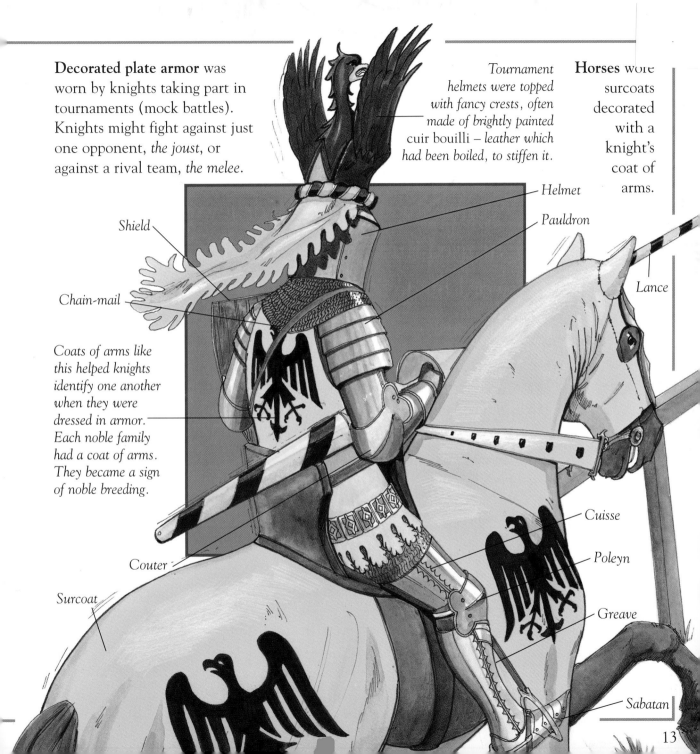

**Decorated plate armor** was worn by knights taking part in tournaments (mock battles). Knights might fight against just one opponent, *the joust*, or against a rival team, *the melee*.

*Tournament helmets were topped with fancy crests, often made of brightly painted cuir bouilli – leather which had been boiled, to stiffen it.*

**Horses** wore surcoats decorated with a knight's coat of arms.

Shield

Chain-mail

*Coats of arms like this helped knights identify one another when they were dressed in armor. Each noble family had a coat of arms. They became a sign of noble breeding.*

Helmet

Pauldron

Lance

Cuisse

Poleyn

Greave

Couter

Surcoat

Sabatan

13

# A knight's most highly prized weapon

was his sword. It was made of iron, with a double-edged blade. Sometimes the handle was decorated with carvings or jewels. In battle, a knight used his sword to slash his enemy. The sword blade had to be very sharp.

Knights also fought with lances (long spears), maces (spiked wooden clubs), and battle-axes. All of these weapons could inflict deadly injuries. In hand-to-hand fighting, knights used daggers to stab their enemies. The sharp point of the dagger could slip between the armor plates.

**Left:** Long sword and half (short) sword, both double-edged. **Right:** Battle-axe and mace.

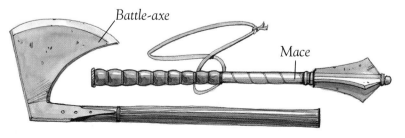

Battle-axe

Mace

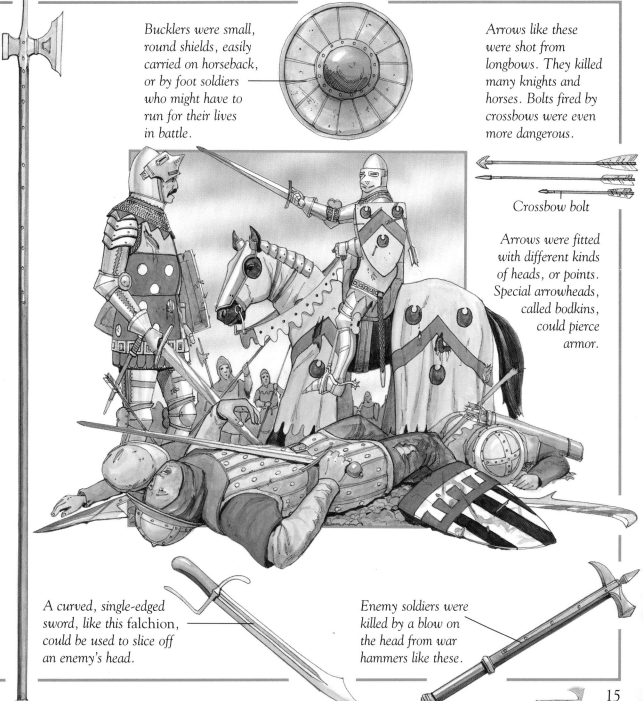

Bucklers were small, round shields, easily carried on horseback, or by foot soldiers who might have to run for their lives in battle.

Arrows like these were shot from longbows. They killed many knights and horses. Bolts fired by crossbows were even more dangerous.

Crossbow bolt

Arrows were fitted with different kinds of heads, or points. Special arrowheads, called bodkins, could pierce armor.

A curved, single-edged sword, like this falchion, could be used to slice off an enemy's head.

Enemy soldiers were killed by a blow on the head from war hammers like these.

**Chain-mail** armor was pulled on over the head. Coats-of-plates (metal plates fixed to a cloth jacket) were fastened by buckles at the back. Underneath, a knight wore a padded tunic.

# Knights relied on skilled craftworkers to get them ready to fight. Blacksmiths made harness fittings and iron shoes for war-horses. Swordsmiths and cutlers made swords and sharp blades. Armorers made all kinds of metal weapons and armor, plus helmets and metal hats, called sallets, for soldiers. Leatherworkers made buckskin tunics, as well as leather gauntlets (gloves), boots, and shoes. Embroiderers made flags for knights to carry into battle.

*Painted shield*

**Helmets** were padded with fabric or wool. Some knights grew their hair long to give padding at the back of the neck.

**After 1300,** sword blades were not flat, like knives. Instead, they were made with a diamond-shaped cross-section. This made them easier to thrust deep into an enemy's flesh.

**A sword** with a sharp, tapered point could burst apart the links in a chain-mail coat.

**Chain-mail** was made of wire rings fastened together with tiny rivets. A mail coat could weigh 20 pounds.

**Armorers** used pliers and hammers to join the links in a coat of mail. This was a slow, careful job.

**It took** a long time to learn how to become an armorer. Apprentices trained for five or seven years.

Hammer

Metal links

Warhorses were specially bred to be strong enough to carry a knight in armor, and to be brave and obedient. A top-class warhorse cost at least as much as a good car today. Rich knights would own at least two. They would also have bold horses for tournaments, lighter and faster horses for hunting, slow-moving "palfreys" for long journeys and packhorses to carry heavy loads.

*Curb bit*

**Warhorses** were controlled by curb bits and were protected by special armor that covered their head and neck.

**Knights** employed grooms to feed and care for their horses. Grooms often slept in the stables, keeping warm in the straw and hay.

**Army baggage** was carried in heavy carts. Knights did not ride in the carts – only women, children, and peasants did that.

# Knights setting off to fight in enemy territory had to take all kinds of supplies with them – weapons, armor, tents, bedding, medicines, spare horses, axes to cut wood for campfires, clean clothes, and stocks of food.

**Often** a priest traveled with the army, setting up a portable altar and saying prayers in the army camp. Women cooked the food.

Cart

Where possible, armies on campaign hoped to buy, or steal, food for themselves and their horses from enemy villages and towns as they passed by. Looting was against the rules of war, but it often happened.

**Knights** carried treasures, like gold and silver coins, or armor and weapons, in strong wooden chests.

**After they had** taken all they needed, looting soldiers set fire to fields and farms so enemy civilians would starve.

*Knights faced sharp-tipped arrows, which came hurtling through the air from enemy bowmen up to 900 feet away.*

# Knights fought on horseback and on foot. On horseback, knights rode side-by-side, in close formation, charging toward the enemy. They hoped to spear them with long, sharp lances or knock them to the ground.

Shield

Knights fought on foot when there was no room to ride. They grouped themselves into a close huddle, brandishing their long, sharp swords. Other footsoldiers – pikemen, longbowmen, and crossbowmen – fought nearby.

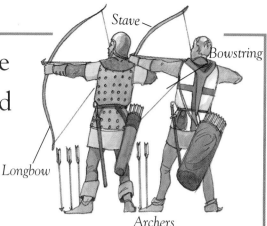

*Stave*

*Bowstring*

*Longbow*

*Archers*

**Longbows** were simple but effective weapons. They were made of a stave (strip) of yew-tree wood. Bowstrings were made of hemp – a plant fiber. It took a force of about 80 pounds to draw the string.

*Lance*

A battering ram smashed down doors.

Siege towers helped attacking soldiers climb over walls.

24

# During a siege, an attacking army

surrounded an enemy castle or town. They knew that food would run out and the enemy would starve. While they were waiting, attackers tried to batter their way through the town or castle walls, using machines called siege engines. They climbed the walls with ladders, or tunneled underneath them.

Bolt

A mangonel was like a massive catapult, firing huge bolts.

Trebuchets hurled huge rocks over defenders' walls.

**Toward the end** of the Middle Ages, cannons were used to break down walls.

**Knights** and ordinary soldiers volunteered to join a crusading army. They believed it was their religious duty.

*Armies traveled to the Holy Land by marching through Europe, or by sailing across the Mediterranean Sea in ships like these.*

# The Crusades were a series of wars, fought between Christian and Muslim armies. Each army wanted control of the Holy Land. The Crusades started in 1095 and continued, on and off, until 1453.

There were Crusades against non-Christian peoples in Europe, too, like the German Pagans and the Jews.

**The Holy Land** included parts of present-day Israel, Syria, Jordan, and Palestinian lands. Jerusalem was the capital – a holy city to Christians, Jews, and Muslims.

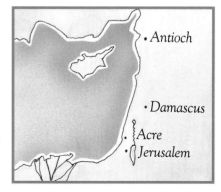

**Pages** helped knights get dressed in armor and in everyday clothes.

Boys from noble families began training to become knights when they were about seven or eight years old. They were sent away from home to live in another noble household, usually belonging to relatives or friends. There, they worked as pages – waiting at table, running messages for the lord and lady, and learning all the rules of polite behavior in noble society. They also learned how to ride. By watching the soldiers all around them, pages learned what a knight's life was like.

*Fake sword*

**Knights** had to be strong. So pages played at fighting using heavy, fake swords. This helped their muscles develop.

*Weight*

*Quintain*

*Shield*

**Knights** practiced fighting at the quintain. It spun around and hit them if they did not get out of the way quickly.

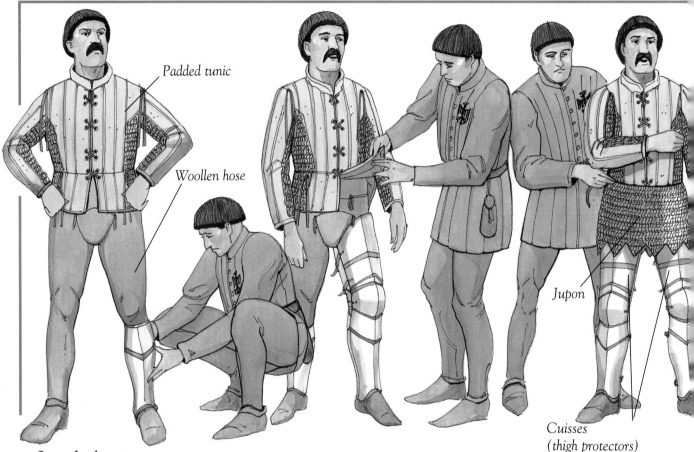

Padded tunic

Woollen hose

Jupon

Cuisses
(thigh protectors)

**It took** almost an hour for a squire to dress his knight in plate armor. Each separate piece had to be tied on to a padded cloth tunic, which the knight wore underneath.

When a page was about 14 years old, he became a squire. He learned all kinds of essential skills – how to use weapons, how to wrestle, how to shoot with a bow and arrow, and how to wear and care for armor.

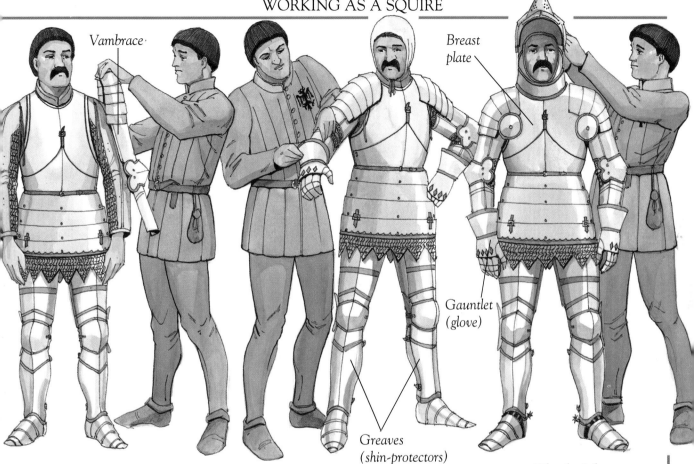

Vambrace

Breast plate

Gauntlet (glove)

Greaves (shin-protectors)

He learned battle tactics and the rules of war, how to look after horses and how to help his lord get ready for a fight. A squire might also serve at the lord's table and entertain guests with poems and songs.

**The knight** wore hose to protect his legs. He bandaged his knees to stop the metal from rubbing against them. Getting dressed began with the feet and ended with the helmet.

Chapel altar

*The squire was dressed in a monk's robe while he said his prayers.*

**The squire's** special bath was meant to clean his body and wash away any sins from his soul. Then he could make a fresh start as a knight.

*Bath water was heated in a huge metal pot. Bath tubs were lined with cloth to protect bathers from splinters.*

**After his bath,** the squire put his weapons on the chapel altar overnight so they would be blessed.

A squire became a knight when he was about 21 years old. Special ceremonies – which took almost 24 hours – marked the beginning of his new life. First, he had a bath. Then he spent the night praying in

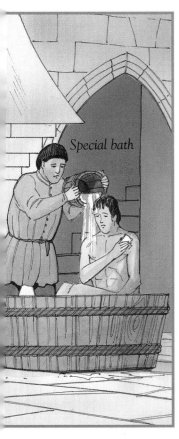

Special bath

Dubbing ceremony

**After being** dubbed, the knight was given a new sword to wear.

**All knights** had the right to be called "sir." If they came from a noble family, they might have the right to other titles, like duke, earl, or count.

**After the** ceremony there was a feast with music and dancing.

the castle chapel. The next morning, the squire was "dubbed" – tapped on the shoulder with a sword by the king or a lord. Now he had new duties and a new rank in life.

*Spurs were a sign of knighthood. They were often given as reward for bravery.*

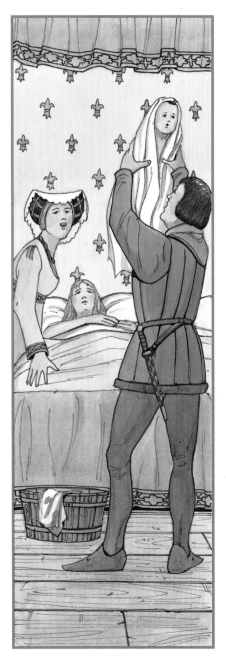

In wartime, kings, lords, and knights relied on their wives to run their estates while they were away. Noblewomen were trained to manage households, keep accounts, and in peacetime, to act as hostesses to important guests. Noblewomen often arranged marriages for their children. Marriage was a way of joining together the riches of ruling families. Brides brought land or goods to their new husbands.

**A noblewoman's** most important duty was to give birth to a son and heir. Noblewomen married young – often before they were 14. Many died in childbirth.

**The church** taught that it was rich peoples' duty to give to the poor. Knights and ladies gave money to beggars, and to orphanages and hospitals run by nuns.

*Noblewomen were responsible for young children's education.*

**Some young knights** fell in love with noble ladies. They praised these ladies in "courtly" poems and songs. Love songs and love stories were popular with noble people in medieval times.

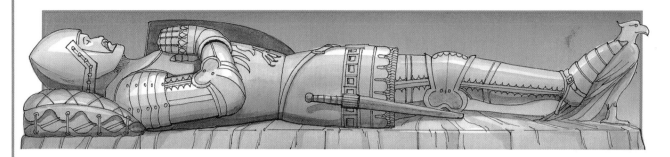

It was rough and dangerous being a knight. Many knights were killed in battle, or died a few days later from infected wounds. Soldiers on campaign in the Middle East risked dysentery and sunstroke. In northern Europe, they faced frostbite and death from cold. Prisoners might catch jail fevers, and killer infections such as the "Black Death" were all around. Knights who survived battles might suffer from their injuries for the rest of their lives.

**Many knights** wanted to make sure they were remembered after their death. They gave money to churches and monasteries for memorial prayers and paid for decorated tombs.

**A fine funeral** was important. Knights' families paid for candles, mourners, funeral music, and priests to watch over the corpse and say prayers. If a knight died abroad, his body might be pickled in brandy and sent home.

# USEFUL WORDS

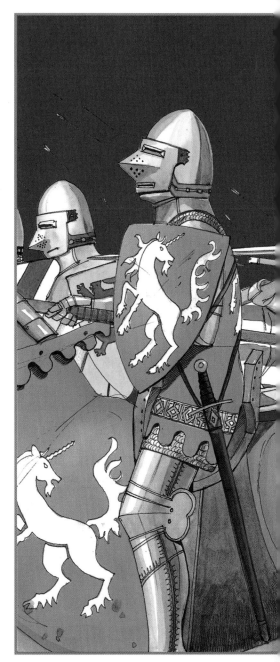

**Aketon** Padded tunic worn under armor.

**Black Death** A deadly disease (the bubonic plague) caused by bacteria (germs). It killed millions of people in Europe and Asia in the 14th and 15th centuries.

**Buckler** Small round shield.

**Chain-mail** Armor made of metal rings linked together.

**Coat of arms** Badge or crest worn by a knight, showing he belonged to a noble family.

**Crusades** Wars fought between Christians and Muslims for the right to rule the Holy Land.

**Curb bit** Metal bar that goes inside the horse's mouth. It helps the rider control the horse.

**Dubbed** Tapped on the shoulders. Part of the ceremony of becoming a knight.

**Falchion** Curved, single-edged sword.

**Joust** Mock battle, fought by one knight against another.

**Melee** Mock battle fought by teams of knights.

**Palfrey** Horse specially bred to be comfortable to ride.

**Plate armor** Armor made of large pieces of metal, shaped to fit the body.

**Quintain** Machine used for practice fighting. It was made of a wooden pole with a shield at one end and a heavy weight on the other.

**Tournament** Mock battles fought by knights for sport and fun.

# INDEX